antique style
bead accessories

matsuko sawanobori

BEADS
CHIC

Antique Style Beads Accessories
© 2002 by Matsuko Sawanobori

Published by Bunka Publishing Bureau,
3-22-1, Yoyogi Shibuya-ku, Tokyo, 151-8524 Japan

First printing: June 2002

Distributors:
United States: Kodansha Amerika, Inc. through Oxford University Press,
198 Madison Avenue, New York, NY 10016.
Canada: Fitzhenry & Whiteside Ltd.,
195 Allstate Parkway, Markham, Ontario L3R 4T8.
United Kingdom and Europe: Premier Book Marketing Ltd.,
Clarendon House, 52, Cornmarket Street, Oxford OXI 3HJ, United Kingdom.
Australia and New Zealand: Bookwise International Pty Ltd.,
174 Cormake Road, Wingfield, South Australia 5013, Australia.
Asia and Japan: Japan Publications Trading Co., Ltd.,
1-2-1 Sarugaku-cho, Chiyoda-ku, Tokyo, 101-0064, Japan.

ISBN 4-88996-089-9

Printed in Japan

Contents

Instructins for each project can be found on the color pages or at the back of this book.
Before you begin working, be sure to read "Basic Techniques" on p.58, and "Before You Begin" on p.60.

About Beads

The key to making attractive accessories is becoming familiar with the characteristics of the many types of beads, and combining them effectively. Most of the beads used to make the accessories in this book are tiny glass seed beads, and lustrous faceted glass or crystal beads. As accents, we also use designer beads of various shapes, and beads made from materials other than glass C pearl or metal beads, for instance. Once you've chosen a color family for your project, you can add other beads of slightly different hues or transparent beads for a natural effect. We also recommend that you try using vintage beads, which are readily available. They have a special aura and color not found in contemporary beads.

Seed Beads

As their name suggests, seed beads are very small, like seeds. They are also the main type of beads used to make accessories. Most of them are made of glass, and they come in a variety of shapes: round, geometric, long and thin (bugle beads), and in a wide spectrum of colors. The range of sizes is almost as broad, so it is a good idea to string some beads on fishing line or other stringing material before you begin a project. You will then know how many beads you need to cover a centimeter, for instance. You might also ask someone at your local bead store for advice.

Cut-glass & Crystal Beads

Faceted glass beads and crystal beads add brilliance and elegance to accessories. Faceted glass beads (at bottom of photograph) usually have an overall round shape and surfaces with many facets (cuts). They come in a broad range of colors and sizes. Crystal beads (at top of photograph) are also faceted beads, with a brilliance similar to that of diamonds. Crystal bicone beads are particularly beautiful, and are often used in necklaces. Round, rectangular, and teardrop crystal beads are also available. They can be used as accents in accessories made primarily with seed beads, or combined with faceted glass beads.

Designer Beads

Designer beads can be used in many ways — as focal points in necklaces and at the ends of lariats, for instance. Some are round, oval, twisted, or triangular. Others are shaped like flowers or birds. They are available in many colors, sizes, and patterns (marbled, variegated). Designer beads are made of glass, plastic, wood, and other materials. Glass designer beads are most effective when combined with seed beads or faceted glass beads. Select designer beads in the same color family as the other beads you are using, or in a complementary color.

✱Vintage Beads

The term "vintage beads" is used to describe beads manufactured 30-99 years ago. Older beads are referred to as "antique beads." Vintage beads are more durable than antique beads, and are available in colors and styles that are sure to enhance an accessory. Look for them at antique shops or craft stores.

Stones & Pearls

Gemstone beads, made from precious and semiprecious stones (such as garnets, peridots, carnelians, and opals), add richness and depth to accessories. These natural stones harmonize perfectly with glass beads. They are rather expensive, but a few gemstones (or even one) can be very effective.

Pearl beads, with their lovely luster, are also well worth considering. Freshwater pearl beads are inexpensive and beautiful. The majority are gray, but white or pastel freshwater pearl beads are also available.

Metal Beads

For a nice contrast, include a few gold or silver beads in a necklace made from glass beads. You might also want to try making a necklace or bracelet using small metal beads exclusively. Create a strikingly modern piece by replacing the seed beads called for in a particular design with metal beads. Gold and silver beads each have their own special tone color and aura, so those you select should go well with the other colors in your piece.

Rings

Today, rings woven from beautifully colored beads are best sellers at accessory shops. They seem difficult to make, but can be completed in a short time with just a few beads, and are ideal projects for beginners. Use wire, because it is easy to work with. To make sure that the ring is the proper size, try it on before you close the circle. If necessary, add or subtract beads.

SIMPLE WOVEN RINGS

Simple, cylindrical rings made from beads that differ subtly in shape and color are very attractive. They are easy to make, using a basic technique that involves forming intersections with wire on which beads are strung.

❶Supplies

Crystal beads and faceted glass beads (the amount will vary according to ring size, but for example, 10 4-mm crystal beads, 10 4-mm or 7 3-mm faceted glass beads), 5-8 strands seed beads, slightly more than 1m wire

■ If you combine beads that are in the same color family, but vary slightly in tone and transparency, you'll get beautiful results. We suggest using seed beads and adding crystal and/or faceted glass beads as accents. Make adjustments in size by increasing or decreasing the number of seed beads. The rings in the photograph measure about 1.8cm in diameter.

⊙Instructions

1 String 5 crystal beads on center of wire. Add a row of seed beads equal in length to the row of crystal beads, and form intersections with the wire, as shown in drawing below. Keep adding rows of beads until ring is wide enough to fit your finger, inserting rows of crystal and faceted glass beads between rows of seed beads.

(All other beads are seed beads.)

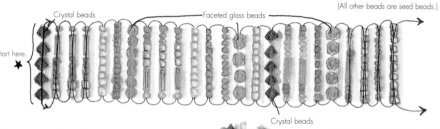

Crystal beads —— Faceted glass beads ——

Start here. ★

Crystal beads

2 Insert wire into first row of crystal beads, as shown in drawing at right. Close the circle, and pass wire through several more rows to secure. Cut excess wire.

★ Work through 2-3 more rows; cut excess wire.

BRACELET

You can use this same technique to make a bracelet. String eight seed beads on center of wire, and proceed as shown in drawing below, adding more seed beads (including bugle beads). Then add one 6-mm crystal bead and one seed bead, pass wire back through crystal bead, and wind around bottom of crystal bead several times.

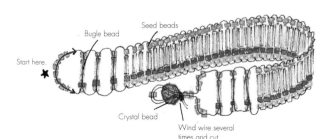

Bugle bead

Seed beads

Start here. ★

Crystal bead

Wind wire several times and cut.

11

RINGS WITH FLORAL MOTIFS

Colored pearl beads, with their soft luster, add a delicate, feminine touch to these rings. We have created a design with a simple floral motif, using pearl beads for the petals, and glass beads for the center of the flower.

❸Supplies

6 4-mm colored pearl beads, 2 3-mm faceted glass beads, seed beads, 50cm wire
- Pearl beads are available in light colors (pink, blue, yellow), and even in dark colors (wine and navy). Use seed beads in the same color family as the pearl beads you select. Ordinary, round 3-mm glass beads can also be used for the centers of the flowers.

⊕Instructions

1 Referring to the drawing below, string pearl beads, faceted glass beads, then pearl beads on the center of the wire. Form intersections with the wire, as shown in drawing below. End with a pearl bead at each edge.

Faceted glass bead   Colored pearl bead   Seed beads

Start here.

2 Form an intersection with the wire in the first faceted glass bead strung, closing the circle. Pass wire through several more patterns to secure. Cut excess wire.

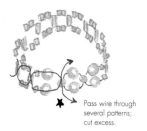

Pass wire through several patterns; cut excess.

✽ V a r i a t i o n

You can produce dramatically different results using this same design if you vary the types of beads used. The ring in the photograph at left is made with garnet beads — a combination of round beads and long, narrow beads.

13

MORE WOVEN RINGS

This basic technique can be applied to many different styles of rings, from the casual to the romantic.

CYLINDRICAL RINGS

Here are two cylindrical rings made with wider beads. The same basic technique is used to make both of them, but the light brown ring has a doughnut shape, while the dark brown ring is more compact.

Instruction on p. 60.

HYDRANGEA RING

This romantic design, suggestive of
hydrangea petals, features
pale blue faceted glass beads,
around which seed beads are scattered
for a decorative touch.

ROSE RING

Round beads are surrounded by
seed beads to make this rose ring.
Be sure to position the petals so
that the finished piece is well balanced.

FLOWER BEAD RING

This ring, which combines small
yellow flower beads and pale green seed beads,
is the perfect spring accessory.

Instruction on p. 61.

15

SILVER WIRE RINGS

These rings are made by stringing beads on silver wire,
while wrapping the wire around a ring stick. For a luxurious look,
add high-quality beads, such as gemstone beads, to create accents.

❶Supplies

A: Flower ring (bottom left of photograph on p. 16)
6 round 4-mm beads for flower petals, 4-mm round bead (use a different color) for center of flower, green 6 x 8-mm oval bead
B: Ring with oval bead (left side of photograph at right)
6 x 8-mm oval bead, 2 4-mm metal beads
C: Ring with circle of beads (right side of photograph at right)
6-mm pebble bead, 4 4-mm round beads
For all rings: 30cm 8-mm silver wire
■ For the rings in the photographs, we used gemstone beads (moonstones, peridots, etc.). You will need a ring stick on which to wrap the wire.

⊙Instructions

1 Wrap wire around a ring stick (or a metal rod with a diameter equivalent to your ring size), leaving a 5-mm end. Pass wire through beads, as shown in drawings below. For Ring A, pass wire through the beads that form the flower, and then through the oval bead, so that it ends up beside the flower.

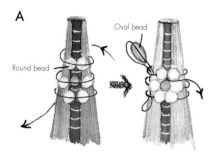

A

Oval bead

Round bead

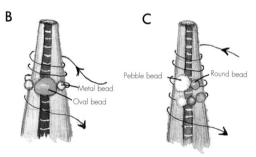

B

Metal bead
Oval bead

C

Pebble bead   Round bead

2 To secure the wire, hold the ring between your fingers next to the beads, and wind each end of the wire around ring several times. Cut excess.

Wind wire several times; cut excess.

✽ V a r i a t i o n

You might want to try a using gemstone beads (garnet, aventurines, etc.) or pearl beads. This is a good technique to use to make a birthstone ring.

Lariats & Necklaces

Lariats can be worn in many different ways. You can wear them like chokers by tying them at the throat. You can also tie them in front, or just let them hang straight. There is no need to attach findings or to worry about making adjustments for size. Necklaces can be made in a wide range of styles — long ropes that wrap twice or three times around your neck, pendants, and chokers, for instance.

SHORT LARIAT WITH POMPOMS

This short lariat with dangling pompoms
is worn tied loosely over the chest. The decorative beads
woven into it sway gently when you move.

❶Supplies (for a 45-cm lariat)

Pompom: 8 5-mm faceted glass beads, 4 4 x 7-mm rice beads (or 5-mm faceted glass beads)

Decorative beads for other end of lariat: 1 each small, medium-sized, and large glass beads

Necklace: Two types of seed beads, preferably bugle beads, in the same color family (one type will serve as accents); 6 rectangular beads (or large seed beads), 2 lengths #3 fishing line (45cm, 1m), 2 crimp beads

■Green beads were used for the accessories in the photographs, but gray or purple also work well.

❷Instructions

1 Make pompom first. Pass 45cm fishing line through faceted glass beads and rice beads, as shown in drawing below. Form an intersection in the first bead, and continue passing fishing line through beads until pompom shape is fully formed and fixed. Cut excess fishing line.

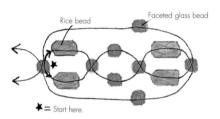

Rice bead
Faceted glass bead
★ = Start here.

2 String a seed bead on 1m fishing line 5cm from end. With fishing line doubled, string decorative glass beads, then a crimp bead. Compress crimp bead with pliers. Cut excess fishing line, and string remaining beads on one strand fishing line. Attach pompom.

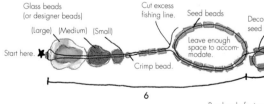

Glass beads (or designer beads)
(Large) (Medium) (Small)
Start here. ✖
Cut excess fishing line.
Seed beads
Crimp bead.
Decorative seed beads
Leave enough space to accommodate.
6

Rectangular beads
8.5
8.5
8.5
5
6.5
6.5
6.5
5

EARRINGS

Insert a head pin into a 5-mm faceted glass bead, as shown in drawing. Add pompom, made as shown above, and then another faceted glass bead. Bend end of head pin into a circle. Insert an eye pin into a faceted glass bead; bend end into a circle. Attach head pin to eye pin, and eye pin to ear wire or earring back.

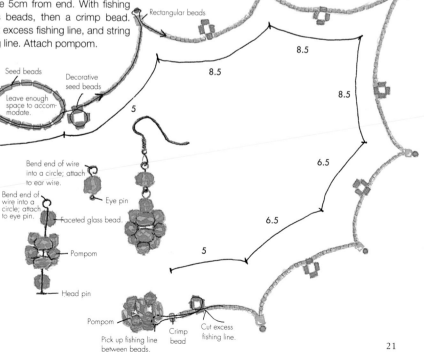

Bend end of wire into a circle; attach to ear wire.
Bend end of wire into a circle; attach to eye pin.
Eye pin
Faceted glass bead.
Pompom
Head pin

Pompom
Pick up fishing line between beads.
Crimp bead
Cut excess fishing line.

LONG LARIAT

One of the nice things about lariats is that they can be worn so many
different ways. This particular lariat, with a bird at one end and a flower
at the other, is made with purple beads. You can substitute the bird and flower
with designer beads of your choice, if you like.

❶Supplies (for a 95-cm lariat)

2 3 x 10-mm glass beads, bird bead (or substitute a large round bead or designer bead), 14 4-mm faceted glass beads, 5 6 x 8-mm oval beads (for flower petals), 6 x 10-mm rice bead, seed beads, two types of bugle beads, 2 head pins, eye pin, 2 lengths #3 fishing line (30cm, 1.5m), 2 crimp beads
■The lariat shown in the photograph was made in shades of purple, a color that is very popular now.

☉Instructions

1 Make a pompom with 30cm fishing line and 12 4-mm faceted glass beads (see p. 21 for instructions). Then make the bird and flower decorations for the ends of the lariat, using head pins and an eye pin, following instructions in drawing below.

2 String seed beads and oval beads on 1.5m fishing line, beginning 13cm from end and following instructions in drawings. String beads for necklace, adding pompom midway. At other end of lariat, pass fishing line through a crimp bead and join to bird bead. Pass fishing line back through beads to crimp bead. Compress crimp bead with pliers, and cut excess fishing line.

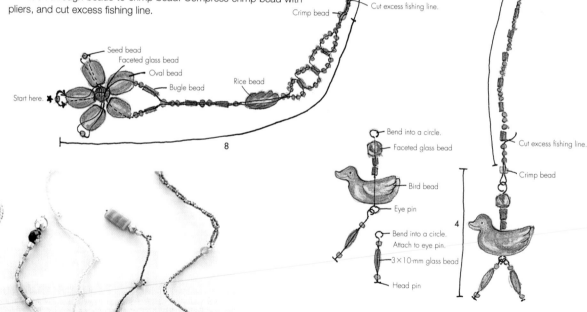

Pompom

83

Cut excess fishing line.

Crimp bead

Seed bead
Faceted glass bead
Oval bead
Bugle bead
Rice bead

Start here.

8

Bend into a circle.
Faceted glass bead

Bird bead

Eye pin

Bend into a circle.
Attach to eye pin.

3×10-mm glass bead

Head pin

Cut excess fishing line.

Crimp bead

4

✸ V a r i a t i o n

If you prefer a simpler design, use large beads at ends of lariat instead of the bird and flower. Oval beads and designer beads shaped like leaves and flowers would work well, too. For a unified look, use beads in complementary colors throughout.

MORE LARIATS

Crystal beads are used as accents in this simple, elegant lariat.
For a streamlined look, choose beads in gradations of one color.

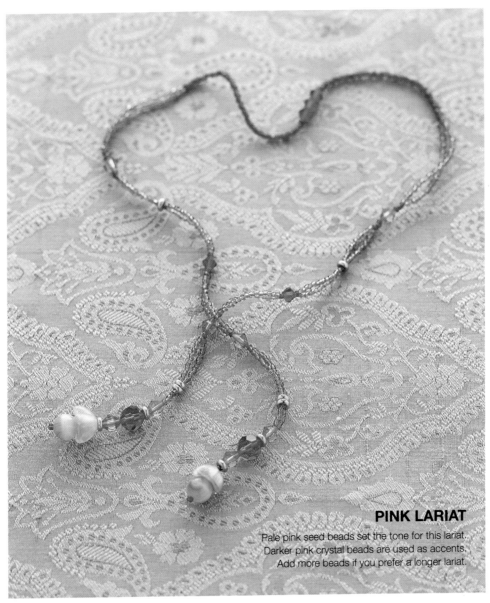

PINK LARIAT

Pale pink seed beads set the tone for this lariat.
Darker pink crystal beads are used as accents.
Add more beads if you prefer a longer lariat.

Instructions on p. 62

SHORT CRYSTAL-BEAD LARIAT

Brilliant crystal beads are the main focus of this dazzling lariat.
Since the beads used are larger than seed beads,
the work goes very quickly.

Instructions on p. 62

25

LONG NECKLACE WITH LARGE ACCENT BEADS

This necklace can be worn doubled or tripled, or at its full length.
Begin with the center, and then work to the left and right in mirror image.

7 large beads, 8 medium-sized beads, 8 small beads, bugle beads, seed beads, slightly more than 1m #3 fishing line, 2 bead tips, 2 crimp beads, 2 jump rings, clasp set
▪For best results, select the large accent beads first and then the smaller ones.

❶**Instructions**

1 String beads onto single strand of fishing line, starting at center and working to left and right in mirror image. Adjust the length of the necklace by increasing or decreasing seed beads at each end.

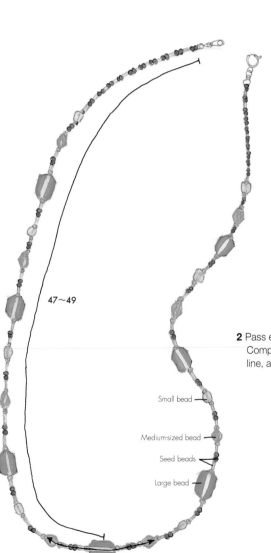

47～49

Small bead

Medium-sized bead

Seed beads

Large bead

★
Start here.

✽ V a r i a t i o n

You can vary this design simply by substituting other types and colors of beads. For instance, you could use metal ethnic beads and blue glass beads, or silver seed beads and round beige beads.

2 Pass each end of fishing line through a bead tip, then a crimp bead. Compress crimp bead with pliers, close bead tip, cut excess fishing line, and attach clasp.

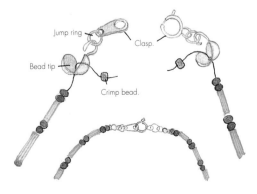

Jump ring

Clasp.

Bead tip

Crimp bead.

NECKLACES WITH PENDANTS

It's easy to weave these simple, attractive pendants.
Pompoms are always a good idea, or you can make square or
heart-shaped pendants. These necklaces will look better
when you wear them if you keep them short.

Crystal beads lend a beautiful
brilliance to this square pendant.
The pendant consists of two squares joined together.
To make it, you simply do a series of repetitions of
the basic weaving technique.

NECKLACE WITH SQUARE PENDANT

28

Instructions on p. 63

NECKLACE WITH
HEART-SHAPED PENDANT

The small heart-shaped pendant is made from
crystal beads, faceted glass beads,
and round beads. For a total look,
make matching earrings.

NECKLACE WITH
POMPOM PENDANT

The pendant is a pompom,
made in two pieces around a large bead.

Instructions on p. 64

Chokers

Chokers made with beautifully colored beads not only enhance what you are wearing, but also light up your face. We encourage you to make one of your own design. There are so many ways to make them — thick woven ropes or cords of beads, beads attached to ribbon — just let your imagination be your guide. Use wire if you prefer a fairly rigid piece, and fishing line for a more natural look.

CHOKERS IN SOFT PASTELS

Chokers made with pastel or transparent beads are perfect for spring and summer. Make the central flower motif first, and then the rest of the choker, working to the left and right.

❷Supplies (for a choker measuring 33-35cm in length)

15 6-mm faceted glass beads, 4 4-mm colored pearl beads, seed beads, 3 lengths wire (1.5m, 2 70-cm lengths), jump ring, lobster or spring clasp

▪Light blue, pink, and lemon yellow beads were used to make the chokers shown in the photograph. Use brown or gray beads for a more subdued look.

ⓘInstructions

1 First, make center section by passing 1.5m wire through faceted glass beads. When center section is completed, bend wire and work back through several patterns. Cut excess. Pass 70cm wire through faceted glass beads to make left side of choker. Repeat on right side. Adjust length of choker by increasing or decreasing the same number of beads at each side.

Choker clasps are often sold in sets that include jump rings. For these chokers, we used only a lobster clasp and one jump ring.

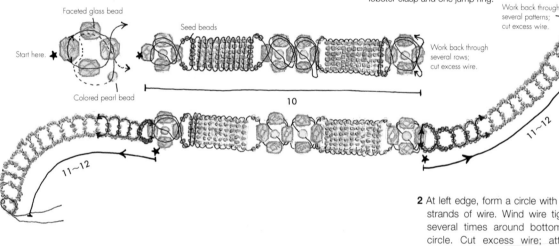

Faceted glass bead

Seed beads

Start here.

Colored pearl bead

Work back through several patterns; cut excess wire.

Work back through several rows; cut excess wire.

10

11~12

11~12

The center section is made first to allow for adjustments in length at each end, and to make the work easier by using shorter lengths of wire.

2 At left edge, form a circle with two strands of wire. Wind wire tightly several times around bottom of circle. Cut excess wire; attach jump ring and clasp to circle. Clasp closes around last circle of beads at other end of choker.

Jump ring

Clasp

Wind wire several times around bottom of circle; cut excess.

DELICATE WOVEN CHOKERS

These delicate woven chokers go particularly
well with youthful fashions. They feature flower motifs and ribbon

CHOKER WITH FLOWER MOTIFS

This romantic choker features flowers made from faceted glass and
crystal beads. It looks complicated to make, but is simply a repetition of the
basic technique. Wire is used to help retain its shape.

Instructions on p. 65

RIBBON CHOKER

Chokers made with ribbon are tied at the back of the neck,
and have a gauzy look. They are made by weaving seed beads into a strip,
which is then attached to organdy ribbon with fishing line.

Instructions on p. 65

FLOWER BEAD CHOKER

This nostalgic design looks wonderful
when worn with a classic suit. Bronze-colored beads are used next
to the flowers and in the clasp, as accents.

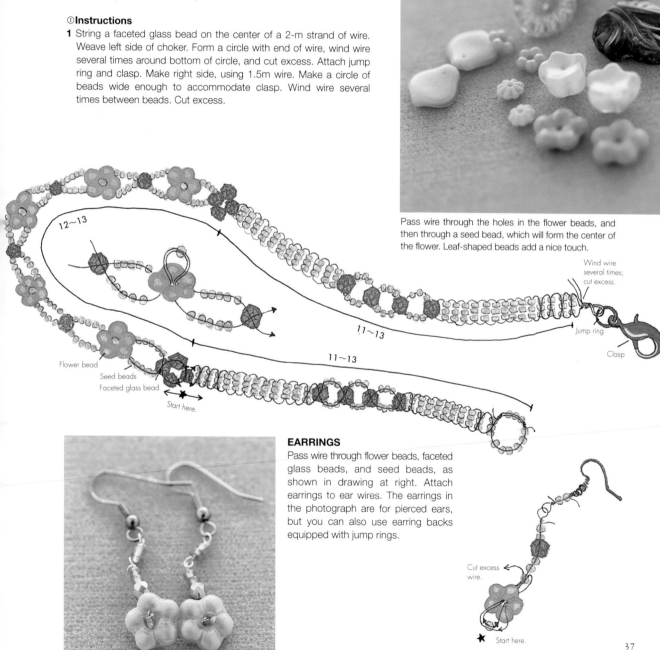

Supplies (for a 35-cm choker)

5 1.5-cm flower beads, bronze (or gold) seed beads, 20 4-mm bronze faceted glass beads, 2 lengths wire (2m, 1.5m), jump ring, lobster clasp

■ Use vintage flower beads, if possible.

Instructions

1 String a faceted glass bead on the center of a 2-m strand of wire. Weave left side of choker. Form a circle with end of wire, wind wire several times around bottom of circle, and cut excess. Attach jump ring and clasp. Make right side, using 1.5m wire. Make a circle of beads wide enough to accommodate clasp. Wind wire several times between beads. Cut excess.

Pass wire through the holes in the flower beads, and then through a seed bead, which will form the center of the flower. Leaf-shaped beads add a nice touch.

12~13

11~13

11~13

Wind wire several times; cut excess.

Jump ring

Clasp

Flower bead

Seed beads

Faceted glass bead

Start here.

EARRINGS

Pass wire through flower beads, faceted glass beads, and seed beads, as shown in drawing at right. Attach earrings to ear wires. The earrings in the photograph are for pierced ears, but you can also use earring backs equipped with jump rings.

Cut excess wire.

★ Start here.

37

MULTI-STRAND CHOKERS

Chokers made from multiple strands,
each one strung with different beads, have a luxurious air about them.
Even if you use beads in the same color family, you can create a striking
effect by using many different types of beads.

❷Supplies (for a 36-cm choker)

14 different types and sizes of gray beads, 35cm fishing line for each strand of choker, clasp set for 3- or 5-strand necklace, 14 60-cm lengths #3 fishing line, 28 crimp beads, 10 bead tips

■Combine different types of beads, such as seed beads, crystal beads, freshwater pearl beads, and metal beads. Other possibilities are gold-toned or blue beads.

⊙Instructions

String 35cm beads on each length of fishing line. Attach a bead tip at each end, and secure with a crimp bead. Cut excess fishing line. Attach 2-4 strands of beads to each bead tip (one if beads are large). Attach bead tips to clasp.

■If you can find a five-strand perforated clasp, use that and decorate it with 3-mm faceted glass beads, as shown below.

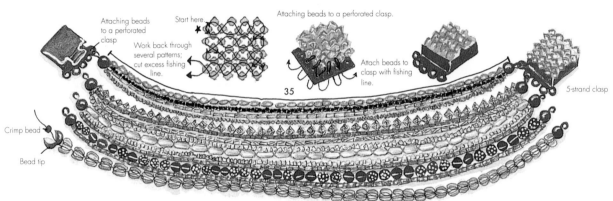

Attaching beads to a perforated clasp

Crimp bead

Bead tip

Start here

Work back through several patterns; cut excess fishing line.

Attaching beads to a perforated clasp.

35

Attach beads to clasp with fishing line.

5-strand clasp

✴ V a r i a t i o n

For a more informal look, use more seed beads. String them on 10 strands fishing line, and attach to an eye pin. Hide fishing line at each end with a bead cap, bend end of eye pin into a circle, and attach clasp.

Add these at intervals for accents.

Crimp bead

Eye pin

Bend end into a circle; attach to clasp.

Clasp.

Bead cap

Choker

FRESHWATER PEARL
BEAD CHOKER

You can make this choker in a very short time,
using a simple weaving method.
Seed beads and silver beads
are used as accents.

40   Instructions on p. 66

SILVER CORD CHOKER

This choker features silver beads. A simple design brings out their best qualities.
Other metal beads or pearl beads (or even seed beads) produce equally nice results.
This choker takes time to make, but presents no difficulties.

Instructions on p. 66

Broochs,
Earrings
Hair Ornaments

Though rings, bracelets, necklaces are the first items that come to mind when you think of beaded accessories, consider adding brooches, earrings, and hair ornaments to your repertoire as well. Special findings, such as perforated pin or earring backs, facilitate the crafting of these pieces. The effect of any accessory is enhanced when you pair it with another matching accessory (earrings and a necklace, or a brooch and a choker, for instance).

SILVER AND GOLD FLOWER BROOCHES

These brooches combine several different types of beads.
They are easy to make. All you do is attach the beads to a perforated
pin back to form the petals of the flower.

For the seven large petals: 5-mm glass beads, 3- and 4-mm faceted glass beads, 4-mm crystal bicone beads

For the seven small petals: 3- and 4-mm faceted glass beads, seed beads, bugle beads

For center of flower: 1-cm faceted glass bead

For both brooches: Wire, crimp bead, 2.4-cm perforated pin back

■Using the above list as a guide, choose gold- or silver-toned beads — larger beads for the large petals, and smaller ones for the small petals.

⊙**Instructions**

1 For the large petals, string 9cm beads on 15cm wire. For the small petals, string 7cm beads on 13cm wire. Wrap wire around base of petals several times. The flower will look more natural if you vary the shapes of the large petals slightly.

2 Pass wire through faceted glass bead that forms center of flower. Then pass wire through perforated pin back, securing it on the wrong side with a crimp bead. Insert large petals into holes on perimeter and in center of pin back, checking to make sure piece is well balanced. Finally, insert small petals into inner holes of pin back.

Perforated pin backs have two sections, top and bottom. The holes are in the top, which is later attached to the bottom.

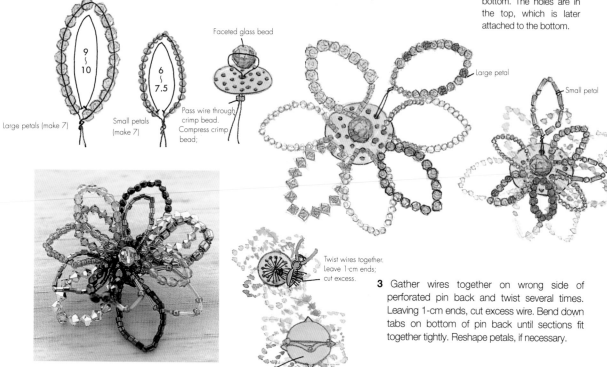

Large petals (make 7)

9～10

Small petals (make 7)

6～7.5

Faceted glass bead

Pass wire through crimp bead. Compress crimp bead;

Large petal

Small petal

Twist wires together. Leave 1-cm ends; cut excess.

Attach bottom of pin back.

3 Gather wires together on wrong side of perforated pin back and twist several times. Leaving 1-cm ends, cut excess wire. Bend down tabs on bottom of pin back until sections fit together tightly. Reshape petals, if necessary.

CORSAGE BROOCH

This brooch is made from a corsage of pastel seed beads.
The sections of the corsage are made separately, and all the wires are gathered
together at the end. We also designed matching earrings.

❶Supplies

Seed beads (white for petals, yellow for petals and center of flower, green for leaves), large green flower bead, 8 small white flower beads, 1.2-cm green round bead, head pin, wire, 10 crimp beads, 1m ribbon, 2.5-cm perforated pin back
■Use seed beads, short bugle beads, or round beads. We recommend narrow ribbon made of organdy or other sheer fabric.

⊙Instructions

1 Make sections of corsage, referring to drawings below. You will need two white flowers, two yellow flowers, five leaves, and eight flowers made from small flower beads (see Fig. 1).

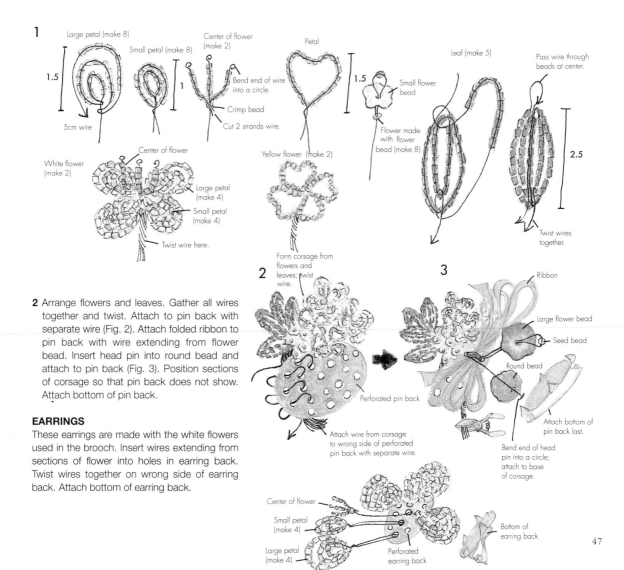

1

Large petal (make 8)

Small petal (make 8)

Center of flower (make 2)

1.5

1

Bend end of wire into a circle.

Crimp bead

5cm wire

Cut 2 strands wire.

Petal

1.5

Leaf (make 5)

Pass wire through beads at center.

Small flower bead

Flower made with flower bead (make 8)

2.5

Twist wires together.

White flower (make 2)

Center of flower

Large petal (make 4)

Small petal (make 4)

Twist wire here.

Yellow flower (make 2)

Form corsage from flowers and leaves; twist wire.

Ribbon

Large flower bead

Seed bead

Round bead

Perforated pin back

2

Attach wire from corsage to wrong side of perforated pin back with separate wire.

3

Attach bottom of pin back last.

Bend end of head pin into a circle; attach to base of corsage.

2 Arrange flowers and leaves. Gather all wires together and twist. Attach to pin back with separate wire (Fig. 2). Attach folded ribbon to pin back with wire extending from flower bead. Insert head pin into round bead and attach to pin back (Fig. 3). Position sections of corsage so that pin back does not show. Attach bottom of pin back.

EARRINGS

These earrings are made with the white flowers used in the brooch. Insert wires extending from sections of flower into holes in earring back. Twist wires together on wrong side of earring back. Attach bottom of earring back.

Center of flower

Small petal (make 4)

Large petal (make 4)

Perforated earring back

Bottom of earring back

MONOCHROME BROOCHES

These simple, elegant brooches are made with one or
two types of beads, all of the same color. It is best to keep the shapes
as simple as possible (square or round, for instance).

RECTANGULAR BROOCH

This brooch features crystal bicone beads woven
into a rectangular shape. For best results, pull on
the fishing line from time to time, so that its tension
remains consistent. Adjust the number of beads to
the size of pin back you have selected.

Instructions on p. 67

ROUND BROOCH

This brooch is made with faceted glass beads.
The beads are woven loosely on fishing line,
which is then inserted into a perforated pin back.
Fishing line should be the same
color as the beads.

SILVER BROOCH

The beads in this lovely brooch sway gently
when you move. A combination of long bugle
beads and faceted glass beads, it is made in the
same way as the round brooch shown above.

Instructions on p. 67

EARRINGS

These simple, chic earrings are sure to become a staple of
your accessory collection. They are easy to make, and the work goes
quickly. These are ideal projects for beginners.

CLUSTER EARRINGS

These clip-on earrings are made by stringing
beads on fishing line to form circles,
which are then attached to
perforated earring backs.

Instructions on p. 68

HANGING EARRINGS

The design for these earrings is based on a simple flower motif.
The transparent fishing line on which the beads are strung gives them
a diaphanous look. The earrings shown in the photograph are for pierced ears,
but they can also be attached to standard earring findings.

Instructions on p. 69

BARRETTE AND COMB

Beaded hair ornaments have become fashionable again.
You might want to try making a barrette or comb using vintage beads.

BARRETTES WITH AN ANTIQUE LOOK

Beads are woven to fit the barrette back,
and then attached to it with wire.

Antique embroidered mirror courtesy of Matild in the Garret

Instructions on p. 69

Combs and hairpins lend themselves to all sorts of designs.
You can weave seed beads or crystal beads and attach them to combs,
or decorate a hairpin with one beautiful bead (or a combination of beads).

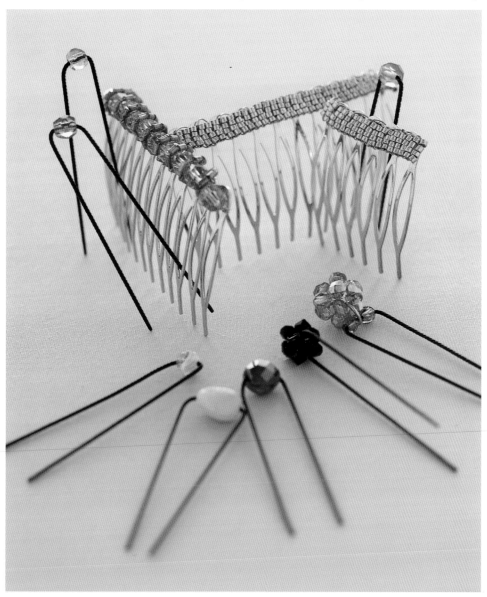

Instructions on p. 70

BLACK-AND-RED POCHETTE

This elegant pochette is worked with red beads on a black background. We have chosen faceted glass beads for this design. The pochette is made in two sections, which are then joined together.

❷Supplies (pochette measures 7 x 7cm)

Pochette: 562 4-mm faceted glass beads (or round beads), 120 3mm garnet beads (or round red beads)

Pompoms: Faceted glass beads (24 4-mm beads, 2 6-mm beads)

Necklace: Seed beads, 20 4-mm faceted glass beads, 22m #3 fishing line

■ All beads are black, with the exception of the garnet beads.

⊕Instructions

1 Make pochette first. Weave two square motifs with faceted glass beads and garnet beads, using 3m fishing line for each (see large drawing and Fig. 1 below). Join bottom and sides of motifs, using 1m fishing line and adding more faceted glass beads. Work back through several patterns; cut excess fishing line (Fig. 2).

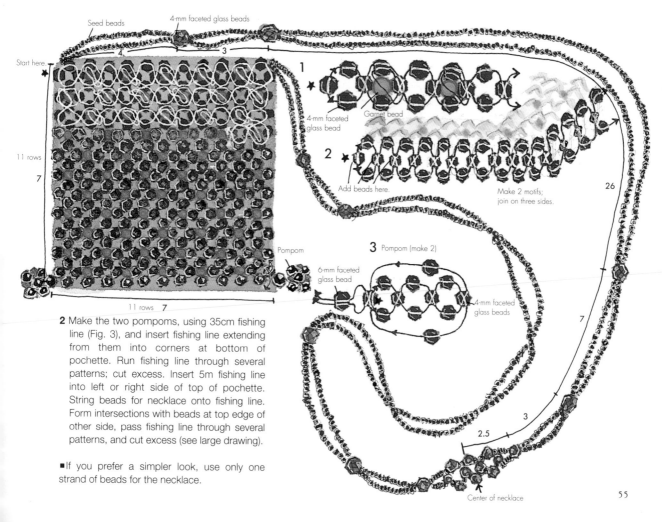

Seed beads

4-mm faceted glass beads

Start here.

4

3

1

4-mm faceted glass bead

Garnet bead

11 rows

7

2

Add beads here.

Make 2 motifs; join on three sides.

26

Pompom

3 Pompom (make 2)

6-mm faceted glass bead

4-mm faceted glass beads

11 rows 7

7

3

2.5

Center of necklace

2 Make the two pompoms, using 35cm fishing line (Fig. 3), and insert fishing line extending from them into corners at bottom of pochette. Run fishing line through several patterns; cut excess. Insert 5m fishing line into left or right side of top of pochette. String beads for necklace onto fishing line. Form intersections with beads at top edge of other side, pass fishing line through several patterns, and cut excess (see large drawing).

■ If you prefer a simpler look, use only one strand of beads for the necklace.

MARABOU NECKLACE

For this piece, we used a pure-white marabou
plume and decorative bead dangles. If you decide to use
a different color plume, select beads of the same color.

Instructions on p. 70

Basic
Technique
& How
to
Make

The following pages contain the basic techniques
used to make the accessories in this book,
as well as instructions not provided on color pages.
Be sure to read "Basic Techniques" on p. 58 and
"Before You Begin" on p. 60 before you start work on a project.

Basic Technique

SUPPLIES YOU WILL NEED

1 Chain-nose pliers: These pliers have flat surfaces. They are used to grasp and twist wire, and to compress crimp beads. These are the pliers to use when you work with wire.

2 Round-nose pliers: These pliers have thin, rounded points. They are used to round the ends of eye pins and other findings.

3 Wire-cutters: These are used to cut wire and fishing line.

▪ A ring stick will come in handy when you want to size a ring, or to make a ring using the wire-wrapping technique.

✳About wire and fishing line

Wire and fishing line are the materials most often used for stringing beads. Fishing line is ideal for many types of accessories, because it is transparent (and therefore practically invisible) and easy to work with. The higher the number, the thicker the fishing line. For the projects in this book, we have used #2 and #3 fishing line. Wire is best suited to rings and brooches, because it has tensile strength and can be shaped. For the accessories in this book, we have used #30 stainless-steel wire, which is resistant to breakage and does not rust. If you're working on a complex piece, and find it difficult to work with a long length of fishing line or wire, cut the material to a comfortable length before you begin work. When you add a new strand of wire, go back a few patterns or rows and rework them until you reach the point where you ran out of wire.

BASIC BEAD-WEAVING TECHNIQUES

✳Getting started

The basic technique for the projects in this book is as follows: String the first bead on the center of a length of wire or fishing line. Then bend the wire in half and string remaining beads on double wire. You will be forming intersections in the beads with the two strands of wire. Since the wire may pass through the hole in any given bead several times, make sure that the holes are large enough to accommodate the wire before you begin. Don't leave gaps between beads.

✳Finishing woven accessories

After you have formed an intersection in the last bead with wire or fishing line, work back through several patterns, and cut excess wire. This process ensures that the fishing line or wire will not come loose. There is no need to tie wire midway through the work. When you are weaving a ring or other circular piece, work back through several patterns, and cut excess wire (finishing techniques for non-woven accessories are described on the next page).

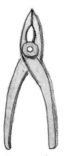
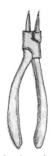

Chain-nose pliers   Round-nose pliers   Wire-cutters

Ring stick

●Start here.

String first bead onto center of wire or fishing line.

●Basic weaving technique

Start here.

Form intersections with wire or fishing line.

Form intersection.

●Finishing

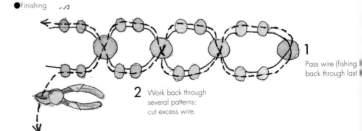

2 Work back through several patterns; cut excess wire.

1 Pass wire (fishing back through last

58

WORKING WITH CRIMP BEADS

When you are stringing beads for a necklace or other non-woven accessory, crimp beads (small metal beads) are used to hold fishing line and other beads in place after they have been compressed with pliers. When you near the end of your work, string a crimp bead onto the fishing line. After you have strung the last bead, compress the crimp bead firmly with pliers. Pass fishing line through a few more beads and cut excess (see drawing at right). Crimp beads are also attached to secure the ends of fishing line when you use bead tips (see next page) or perforated findings.

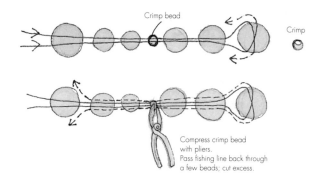

Crimp bead

Crimp

Compress crimp bead with pliers.
Pass fishing line back through a few beads; cut excess.

ATTACHING CLASPS TO NECKLACES

Generally, necklace clasps come in sets consisting of a lobster or spring clasp and a jump ring or chain tab. Normally, a clasp is attached to a bead tip (see drawings below). Bead tips are used to hold the end of the fishing line in place and to connect the beads and the clasp. If you use a bead tip, attach a small jump ring to it, and then attach the jump ring to the clasp.

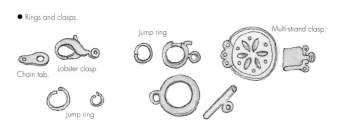

● Rings and clasps.

Chain tab.
Lobster clasp
Jump ring
Multi-strand clasp
Jump ring

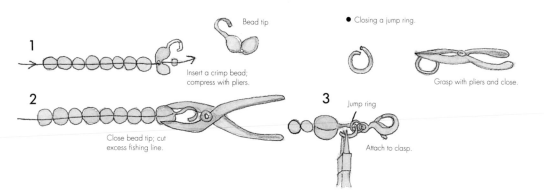

1
Bead tip

Insert a crimp bead; compress with pliers.

● Closing a jump ring.

Grasp with pliers and close.

2
Close bead tip; cut excess fishing line.

3
Jump ring

Attach to clasp.

WORKING WITH HEAD PINS AND EYE PINS

Head pins and eye pins are used to join beadwork to earring findings, or to other sections of a piece. Use head pins when you're joining beadwork at one end only, and eye pins when you're joining beadwork at both ends. If you're simply bending the end of one of these pins down, use your hands. If you're forming it into a circle, use round-nose pliers.

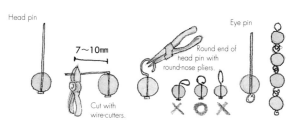

Head pin

Eye pin

7~10mm

Cut with wire-cutters.

Round end of head pin with round-nose pliers.

H o w   t o   M a k e

BEFORE YOU BEGIN

✱Selecting beads

The specifications for each project (type and number of beads) are intended to serve as a guide. You can use any beads you like, as long as they are the same size as those specified. For instance, you can substitute any type of glass bead for faceted glass or crystal beads. When a design calls for seed beads, you can use either round beads or bugle beads, but you may need to adjust the number to allow for slight differences in size. When you purchase beads, either consult with a craft store employee, or string a few on fishing line and then measure to see how many you will need. Unless otherwise specified, all beads called for in this book are made of glass.

✱Making adjustments in size

The size of a beaded accessory differs according to the number of beads used and the way they are strung. While you are working on a project, try it on and adjust the number of beads. The easiest way to make slight adjustments is to increase or decrease the number of seed beads. For necklaces worked from the center out (left-right mirror image), make increases or decreases on each side. You can enlarge rings made with wire by placing them on a ring stick.

■All numbers in drawings refer to centimeters. ■The starting point is indicated by a i in all drawings.

CYLINDRICAL RINGS (shown on p. 14)

A. Light brown ring
❶Supplies
32 4-mm light brown faceted glass beads, 64 gold seed beads, 1m wire

B. Dark brown ring
❶Supplies
26 4-mm brown crystal beads, 78 brown seed beads, 1m wire

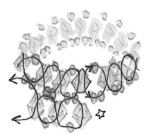

☺Instructions

1 These instructions apply to both A and B. Directions inside parentheses refer to B. Begin by stringing a faceted glass bead (crystal bead) on center of wire. Pass wire through 16 faceted glass beads or 48 seed beads (13 crystal beads or 52 seed beads). Attach end of wire to wire at beginning of work to close the circle.

Faceted glass bead

Start here

Seed bead

A

Crystal bead

B

2 A. Weave next row of beads, as shown in drawing. When row is completed, form an intersection with wire in faceted glass bead at beginning of row (☆). Work back through a few patterns; cut excess wire.

B. Follow directions for A, stringing two seed beads at a time.

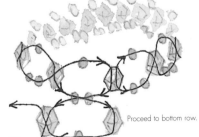

Proceed to bottom row.

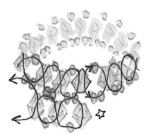

Pass wire through beads at ☆ once again.
Work back through several patterns; cut excess wire.

HYDRANGEA RING (shown on p. 15)
❶Supplies
20 4-mm blue faceted glass beads, 20 purple seed beads (for center of flower), 40 white seed beads, 60cm #2 fishing line
☉Instructions
String three seed beads (for center of flower) on center of fishing line. Begin forming intersections at fourth seed bead. Weave remaining beads, referring to drawing at right. Form intersections in first bead strung, closing the circle. Work back through several patterns and cut excess fishing line.

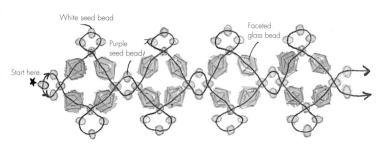

ROSE RING (shown on p. 15)
❶Supplies
7-mm round bead, seed beads (purple for framework of ring, white for petals, green for leaves), 1m wire
☉Instructions
1 Beginning at i, weave beads into a chain until you have enough to fit around your finger. Then make the center framework, on which the rose will be formed. Insert wire into first bead worked, and work back through several beads (see Fig. 1).
2 Attach round bead to center framework (Fig. 2). String beads for petals, then form petals by passing wire through beads in framework. Repeat 6-8 times, making sure the design is well balanced (Fig. 3). Bring wire out next to rose and string green seed beads. Pass wire through beads in framework, forming three leaves (Fig. 4). Wind wire around base of rose; cut excess.

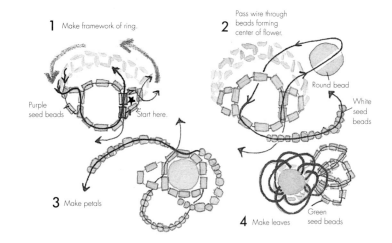

FLOWER BEAD RING (shown on p. 15)
❶Supplies
2 small yellow flower beads, green seed beads, 35cm wire
☉Instructions
String seed beads on wire, forming a chain long enough to fit around your finger (Fig. 1). Pass wire back through beads to starting point (i), forming a circle. Pass wire through beads forming leaves, and then through flower beads (Fig. 2). Wrap wire around base of flower several times, then pass through a few adjacent beads, and cut excess.

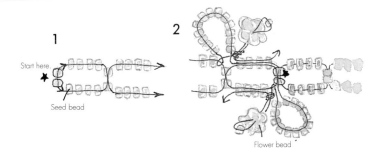

PINK LARIAT (shown on p. 24)
❶Supplies
2 8-mm round beads, 2 8-mm flower beads, 2 dark pink 8-mm crystal beads, 5 dark pink 5-mm crystal bicone beads, 8 6-mm pale pink crystal beads, 10 small metal beads, seed beads (red, pale pink), 1.3m #3 fishing line, crimp bead

■Beads are pale pink unless otherwise specified.

⊙Instructions
1 String seed beads on center of fishing line. Weave as shown in drawing. Work from the center to the left and right, in mirror image.

2 Several beads from the end, string a crimp bead on fishing line. Once the last seed bead has been strung, pass fishing line back through work up to and including crimp bead. Compress crimp bead; cut excess fishing line.

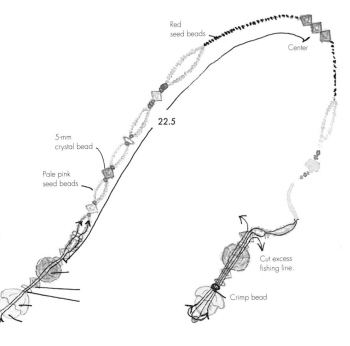

Red seed beads

Center

22.5

5-mm crystal bead

Pale pink seed beads

Cut excess fishing line.

Crimp bead

SHORT CRYSTAL-BEAD LARIAT (shown on p. 25)
❶Supplies
2 8-mm crystal cube beads (or designer beads), 2 6-mm faceted glass beads, 2 4-mm faceted glass beads, 2 8-mm crystal beads, 120 4-mm crystal bicone beads, 2 seed beads, 1.2m #3 fishing line, crimp bead

⊙Instructions
String a seed bead on center of fishing line. String remaining beads, referring to drawings at left. When all 4-mm crystal beads have been strung, string crimp bead, and then remaining beads. Pass fishing line back through crimp bead. Compress crimp bead, pass fishing line back through several more beads, and cut excess fishing line.

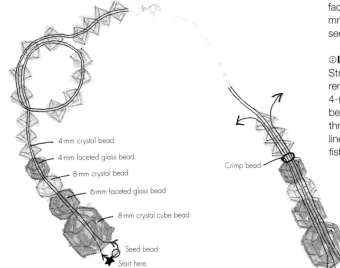

4-mm crystal bead

4-mm faceted glass bead

8-mm crystal bead

6-mm faceted glass bead

8-mm crystal cube bead

Seed bead

Start here.

Crimp bead

End here.

NECKLACE WITH SQUARE PENDANT (shown on p. 28)

❶Supplies (pendant measures 2 x 2cm)

Pendant: 48 4-mm crystal bicone beads, 24 seed beads
Necklace: 1 8-mm crystal bead, 4-mm crystal bicone beads, seed beads, crimp bead, bead tip, 2 jump rings, clasp set, #3 fishing line (1.2m, 2 1-m lengths)

❷Instructions

1 First, make the pendant. Pass fishing line through 4-mm crystal beads. Weave three rows. Hide end of fishing line and cut excess (Fig. 1). Make another identical piece.

2 String two seed beads onto center of 1.2m fishing line. Place half of pendant on top of other half, and pass fishing line through beads in one of the corners. Continue joining halves adding two seed beads each time, until you have joined all four sides (Fig. 2). Work back to the starting point (i in Fig. 2), and form an intersection in the beads there. String seed beads and crystal beads until necklace is desired length, referring to Fig. 3. Attach a bead tip, crimp bead, and clasp to ends of necklace.

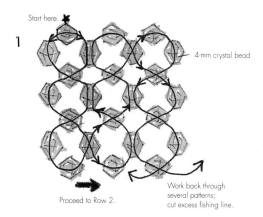

1

Start here.

4-mm crystal bead

Proceed to Row 2.

Work back through several patterns; cut excess fishing line.

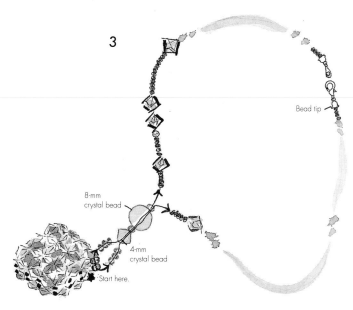

2

Start here.

Weave around edge.

3

8-mm crystal bead

4-mm crystal bead

Start here.

Bead tip

NECKLACE WITH POMPOM PENDANT (shown on p. 29)

❶Supplies (pompom measures 1.5cm in diameter)

Pompom: 15 4-mm black faceted glass beads, 30 black seed beads, 1 8-mm transparent faceted glass bead, 2 60-cm lengths #2 fishing line

Necklace: 3-mm black faceted glass beads, transparent seed beads, #3 fishing line, 2 crimp beads, 2 bead tips, 2 jump rings, clasp set

⊙Instructions

1 Make half of pompom, using 60cm fishing line (Fig. 1).

2 String five seed beads on 60cm fishing line. Make second half of pompom, picking up faceted glass beads on outer edge of first half as you go along (Fig. 2). Before completing pompom, insert fishing line for necklace strung with a transparent faceted glass bead into it, so that fishing line extends from center of pompom on both sides.

3 String beads for necklace on fishing line extending from pompom until desired length is attained, referring to Fig. 3. Attach crimp beads, bead tips, jump rings, and clasp.

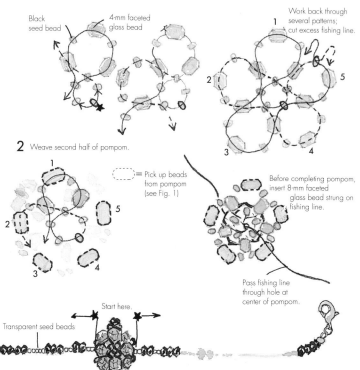

1 Weave first half of pompom.

Black seed bead

4-mm faceted glass bead

Work back through several patterns; cut excess fishing line

2 Weave second half of pompom.

⬭ = Pick up beads from pompom (see Fig. 1)

Before completing pompom, insert 8-mm faceted glass bead strung on fishing line.

Pass fishing line through hole at center of pompom.

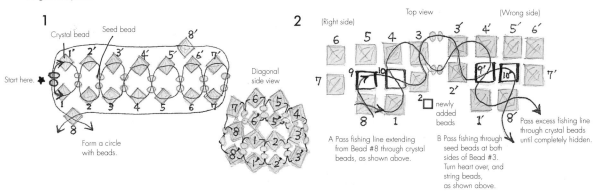

3

Jump ring

Bead tip

3-mm cut glass beads

Transparent seed beads

Start here.

NECKLACE WITH HEART-SHAPED PENDANT (shown on p. 29)

❶Supplies

Pendant: 20 4-mm transparent crystal bicone beads, gray seed beads, 50cm #2 fishing line

Necklace: Beads of the same type and size used for pendant, #2 fishing line, 2 bead tips, 2 crimp beads, 2 jump rings, clasp set

⊙Instructions

1 String beads on fishing line and make pendant (Figs. 1 and 2). Pass separate strand fishing line through beads at top center of pendant. String beads to form necklace. Attach crimp beads, bead tips, jump rings, and clasp.

1

Crystal bead

Seed bead

Start here.

Diagonal side view

Form a circle with beads.

2

(Right side)

Top view

(Wrong side)

□ = newly added beads

A Pass fishing line extending from Bead #8 through crystal beads, as shown above.

B Pass fishing through seed beads at both sides of Bead #3. Turn heart over, and string beads, as shown above.

Pass excess fishing line through crystal beads until completely hidden.

64

CHOKER WITH FLOWER MOTIFS (shown on p. 34)
❶Supplies (for a choker measuring 34cm in length)
6-mm round crystal beads (5 each navy and purple), 60 4-mm faceted glass beads, 32 6-mm bugle beads, seed beads, 2 1-m lengths wire, 2 jump rings, lobster or spring clasp

■Beads are purple unless otherwise specified.

☉Instructions
Form a small circle at each end of a 1-m double strand of wire. Wind wire several times around bottom of circle. Weave choker, referring to drawings below. Attach a jump ring to each end, and the clasp to one end.

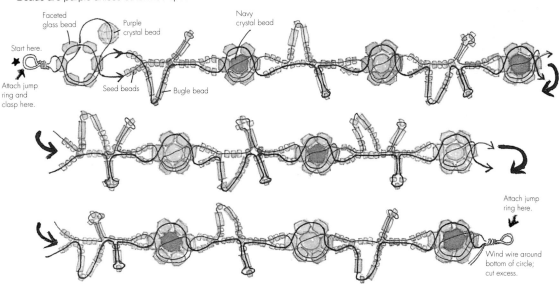

RIBBON CHOKER (shown on p. 35)
❶Supplies (for a 90-cm choker)
Black seed beads, 2 black teardrop crystal beads, 90cm 8-mm gray organdy ribbon, 4 lengths #3 fishing line (2m, 50cm, 2 5-cm lengths)

☉Instructions
1 String seed beads on 2m fishing line. Weave two rows. When piece is 16cm long, work back through several patterns and cut excess wire.
2 Place woven seed beads on center of ribbon. Insert fishing line into ribbon from wrong side, picking up fishing line between beads. Bring fishing line out on wrong side. Repeat until beads are secured to ribbon. Pass both ends of fishing line back between beads; cut excess. Pass 5cm fishing line through crystal beads. Sew to ends of ribbon; tie ribbon.

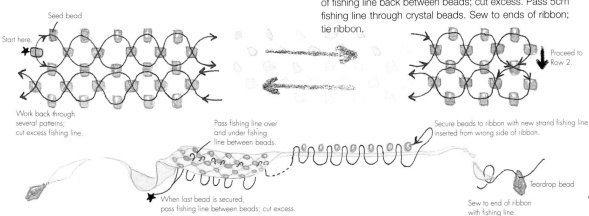

FRESHWATER PEARL BEAD CHOKER (shown on p. 40)
❷Supplies (for a 35-cm choker)

72 small white (or gray) freshwater pearl beads, 64 large seed beads (same color as pearls), 28 silver (or use a contrasting color) beads or round seed beads, 2m wire, 2 jump rings, clasp set

■The numbers of beads specified above are simply a guide, since they will change according to the size of beads used.

⊙Instructions

Bend wire in half. Grasp the bend and twist it several times, forming a small circle. Weave choker, interspersing pearl beads with silver beads or round seed beads (see drawing). Attach a jump ring to each end; attach clasp.

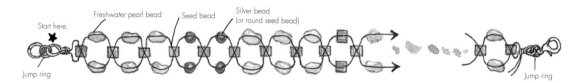

SILVER CORD CHOKER (shown on p. 41)
❷Supplies (for a 35-cm choker)

2-mm silver or other metal beads, 2 lengths #3 fishing line (5m, 45cm), 2 crimp beads, 2 bead caps, clasp set

⊙Instructions

1 Weave three rows of beads, each 31-33cm long, referring to drawings. Weave Row 4, picking up the beads from Row 1, one at a time. When you have formed a cylinder, work back through a few beads and cut excess fishing line. Since long strands are hard to work with, cut fishing line into 1-m lengths. If you run out, work back over a few patterns, add new fishing line, and cut old fishing line.

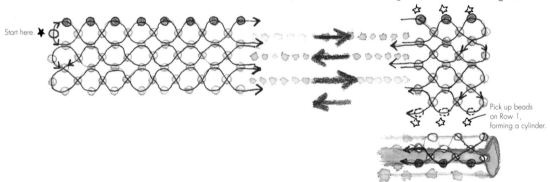

2 Pass 45cm fishing line through choker. Attach a cap, crimp bead, and a metal bead to each end, in that order. Attach clasp. Pass fishing line back through findings to crimp bead. Compress crimp bead; cut excess fishing line.

■A bead cap is a domed finding used to cover the end of the fishing line.

RECTANGULAR BROOCH (shown on p. 48)

⊕Supplies (brooch measures 1.5 x 7cm)
188 4-mm blue crystal bicone beads, 64 gray seed beads, #2 fishing line (1m, 2 1.5-m lengths), pin back (1.5 x 7cm)

⊕Instructions

1 String crystal beads on 1.5m fishing line and weave three rows of 13 patterns each. Work back through a few beads; cut excess fishing line. Make another identical piece.

2 String two seed beads on center of 1m fishing line. Place one half of brooch on top of other half. Join two halves by passing fishing line through bead in a corner of the first half, adding two seed beads at a time. When you reach the starting point, work back through a few patterns and cut excess fishing line. Attach brooch to pin back with double-sided tape. Bend down tabs on pin back.

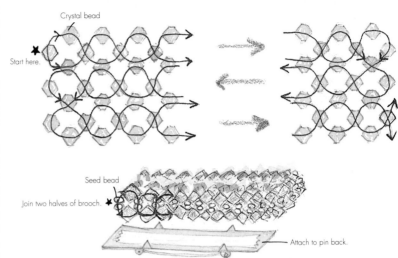

Crystal bead
Start here.

Seed bead
Join two halves of brooch.
Attach to pin back.

ROUND BROOCH (shown on p. 49)

⊕Supplies (brooch measures 4cm in diameter)
Purple faceted glass beads (12 4-mm beads, 10 5-mm beads, 26 6-mm beads), 2 lengths #2 fishing line (2.5m, 50cm), 2.4-cm perforated pin back, 2 crimp beads

⊕Instructions

1 Fold 2.5m fishing line in half. Tie fishing line loosely, adding a faceted glass bead every two loops. Continue until you have used all the beads (Fig. 1).

2 Pass 50cm fishing line through a perforated pin back from the wrong side. Secure woven piece to pin back by picking up fishing line from woven piece in several locations. Pass fishing line through every hole in the pin back until brooch is round in shape. Attach a crimp bead to wrong side of pin back. Compress crimp bead, cut excess fishing line, and bend down tabs on pin back (Fig. 2).

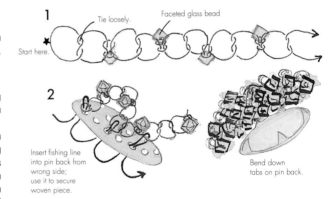

1
Tie loosely.
Faceted glass bead
Start here.

2
Insert fishing line into pin back from wrong side; use it to secure woven piece.
Bend down tabs on pin back.

SILVER BROOCH (shown on p. 49)

⊕Supplies (brooch measures 7cm in diameter)
Faceted glass beads (20 3-mm beads, 60 4-mm beads), 80 2-cm bugle beads, 80 head pins, 2 lengths #2 fishing line (4m, 50cm), 2.4-cm perforated pin back, 2 crimp beads
■All beads are gray.

⊕Instructions

1 Insert head pin into a faceted glass bead and a bugle bead. Bend end of pin into a double circle. Make 80 of these. Tie 4m fishing line, following directions for round brooch shown above. Inserting a head pin every centimeter (every two loops), as shown in Fig. 1.

2 Attach brooch to perforated pin back with 50cm fishing line, making sure brooch is well balanced (Fig. 2). Attach bottom half of pin back.

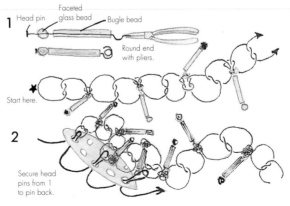

1
Head pin
Faceted glass bead
Bugle bead
Round end with pliers.
Start here.

2
Secure head pins from 1 to pin back.

CLUSTER EARRINGS (shown on p. 50)
FRESHWATER PEARL BEAD EARRINGS
❶Supplies (earrings measure 1.5cm in diameter)
Freshwater pearl beads (22 small, 24 medium, 2 large), 3 lengths #3 fishing line (1m, 2 5-cm lengths), 4 crimp beads, 1.5-cm perforated earring backs
■Adjust the number of beads to size of earring back.

☺Instructions
Attach large freshwater pearl bead to earring back with 5cm fishing line (Fig. 1). String medium-sized pearl beads on 1m fishing line and form a circle (Fig. 2). With same strand of fishing line, attach pearl beads to earring back by picking up fishing line between them (Fig. 3). Attach remaining pearl beads in same way (Fig. 4). Attach a crimp bead to wrong side of earring back. Attach bottom of earring back (Fig. 5).

BRONZE EARRINGS (shown on p. 50)
❶Supplies (earrings measure 2.4cm in diameter)
70 4-mm bronze faceted glass beads, 5 lengths #3 fishing line (1m, 4 5-cm lengths), 4 crimp beads, 2.4-cm perforated earring backs

☺Instructions
These earrings are made in the same way as the freshwater pearl bead earrings. Secure beads to perforated earring backs, working two rows, as shown in drawings below. Finish by adding a crimp bead to wrong side of earring back. Attach bottom of earring back.

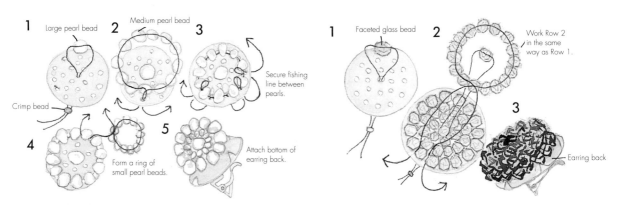

PURPLE EARRINGS (shown on p. 50)
❶Supplies

(earrings measure 2.5cm in diameter)
2 4-mm faceted glass beads, seed beads, bugle beads, small faceted glass beads, 3 lengths #3 fishing line (1m, 2 5-cm lengths), 6 crimp beads, 1.8-cm perforated earring backs

☺Instructions
String a 4-mm faceted glass bead on fishing line. Insert fishing line into earring back (Fig. 1). Bring fishing line out on right side through hole on outer edge. String 2.5cm seed beads, bugle beads, and faceted glass beads on fishing line. Insert end of fishing line into hole in earring back next to center hole. Repeat this process six more times (Figs. 2 and 3). Finish by adding a crimp bead to wrong side of earring back. Attach other half of earring back (Fig. 4).

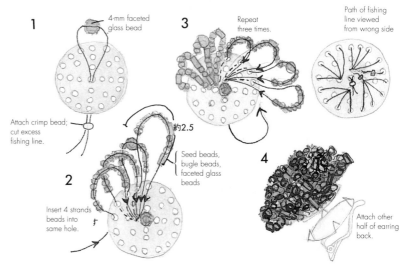

HANGING EARRINGS (shown on p. 51)
WHITE OR PINK EARRINGS
❶Supplies (earrings measure 2.5cm in diameter)
10 5-mm freshwater pearl beads
Center of flower: 3-mm pink faceted glass bead (pink earrings), small freshwater pearl bead (white earrings)
GRAY EARRINGS
16 3-mm gray faceted glass beads, 2 6-mm transparent round crystal beads
■For all three types of earrings you will need 2 40-cm strands #3 fishing line, 2 crimp beads, and ear wires (or earring backs)

①Instructions
For white or pink earrings, see drawings at right. For gray earrings, refer to drawings at left. Weave beads on fishing line; attach ear wires (or earring backs).

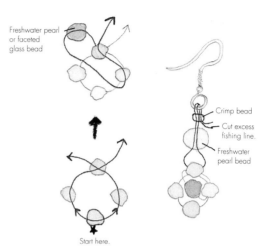

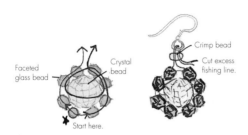

BARRETTES WITH AN ANTIQUE LOOK
(shown on p. 52)
❶Supplies (for 8.5-cm barrette)
15 6-mm faceted glass beads, 4 4-mm faceted glass beads (for center of flower), seed beads, 2 lengths wire (1.5m, 80cm), large barrette back

①Instructions
Weave flower, starting at center of 1.5-m strand wire, and referring to drawing at left. Weave remainder of barrette, referring to drawings at bottom of page. When last bead has been added, work back through several patterns. Cut excess wire. Place woven piece on barrette back and secure with 80cm wire. Pick up beads at edge of woven piece, as shown in drawing, forming intersections on wrong side of barrette back. Insert wire into bead at end of barrette back, wind it around finding where it will not show, and cut excess.

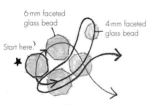

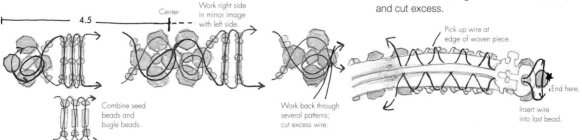

COMBS AND HAIRPINS (shown on p. 53)
GOLD COMB
❶Supplies
10 6-mm crystal beads, seed beads, 60cm wire, comb with 12 peaks

☺Instructions
String 10 crystal beads on wire. Attach to comb, as shown in drawings. Add seed beads, wrapping around comb to secure.

OTHER COMBS AND HAIRPINS
Decorate a comb with seed beads woven into bands (Fig. 1), or a U-pin with your favorite beads (Fig. 2).

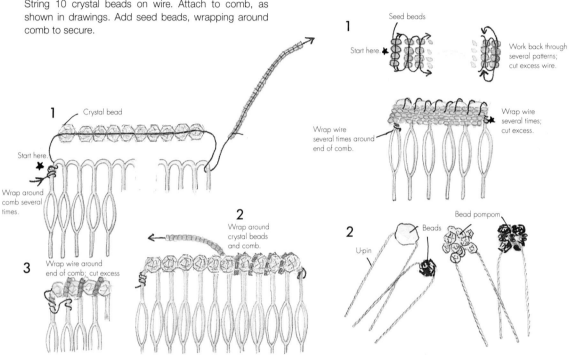

MARABOU NECKLACE (shown on p. 56)
❶Supplies (for a 68-cm necklace)
48-cm marabou plume, 2 8-mm crystal cube beads (or designer or round beads), crystal bicone beads (2 5-mm, 2 8-mm beads), seed beads, 2 25-cm lengths #3 fishing line, 2 bead tips, 2 crimp beads, 2 jump rings, 2 crimps

■We used white beads for the piece shown in the photograph. Crimps are attached to leather or fabric cord, and then to other findings.

☺Instructions
String beads on fishing line, as shown in drawings. Attach crimp to marabou plume.

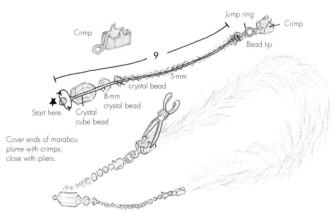

ABOUT THE AUTHOR

Sawanobori Matsuko is a jewelry artist and the owner of a bead shop, Hiroo Bead Bazaar, in Tokyo. Based in New York, she has been designing and creating accessories at her studio, Les Halles, since 1980.

Ms.Sawanobori has won acclaim for her work, designed to complement the latest fashions, both in Japan and abroad. Many of her pieces have been featured in magazines and on television. Currently, she teaches beadcraft at Bunka Fashion College and at her shop.